THE
VENISON
BOOK

AUDREY ALLEY GORTON

ILLUSTRATED BY GEORGE DALY

DOVER PUBLICATIONS, INC.
Mineola, New York

Bibliographical Note

This Dover edition, first published in 2002, is an unabridged republication of *The Venison Book: How to Dress, Cut Up and Cook Your Deer,* first published by The Stephen Greene Press, Brattleboro, Vermont, 1957.

Library of Congress Cataloging-in-Publication Data

Gorton, Audrey Alley.
　　The Venison Book / Audrey Alley Gorton.
　　　　p. cm.
　　Originally published: Brattleboro, Vt. : Stephen Greene Press, 1957.
　　ISBN 0-486-42224-0 (pbk.)
　　　　I. Cookery (Venison). I. Title.

TX751 .G6 2002
641.6'91–dc21   2002017409

International Standard Book Number: 0-486-42224-0

Manufactured in the United States of America
Dover Publications, Inc., 31 East 2nd Street, Mineola, N.Y. 11501

Contents

I GOOD INTENTIONS 7

II SO NOW IT'S VENISON 9
First Catch Your Deer
Hog-dressing the Kill

III BUT IT'S STILL NOT STEAK 21
Out of the Woods
To Hang or Not to Hang
Skinning

IV THE KITCHEN A SHAMBLES 32
Halving
Quartering
Or Do it This Way
Odds and Ends

V KEEP IT YOURSELF 41
Packaging for the Freezer
Pressure Canning
Curing with Salt and Smoke

VI VENISON RECIPES 48
Season to Taste
Marinades
Broiling and Roasting
Some Call it Stew
Fine but Unclassified

VII THE COMPANY IT KEEPS 70
INDEX 78

CHAPTER I

Good Intentions

IN THE GOOD OLD DAYS before the general use of deep-freeze facilities, the fortunate family with a deer at its disposal hacked off the best of the meat, somewhat hazy as to what constituted the "best," gave away as much of the rest as could be made to look familiar or just presentable, and threw away the remainder with a feeling of guilt.

Good meat was going to waste, but what could be done about it? Country people were known to have ways of canning venison, but these methods were considered doubtful if not positively dangerous by summer people. Canned meat, like string beans, was suspect — "botulinus or something. And the worst of it is you can't *taste* it. It's like mushrooms that aren't, and carbon monoxide, you know."

In these days, whether you plan to store it in the home freezer or in rented locker space, there is no reason why all of the deer should not end up on your table. This will mean that you have from fifty to one hundred-plus pounds of meat at a nominal cost. The cost *may* be as low as $2.50 for a hunting license and ten cents for one shell.

This book is intended to help you bring down your deer with the least waste of edible meat, and to get it either to the butcher or into the home freezer in prime condition; and, finally, to suggest various ways to cook and serve it. These operations are by no means so difficult or complicated as they may seem to the uninitiated. However, it does help if you know what you are going to do and why. The procedures in the book are all the results of personal experience.

When I first looked for venison recipes to try, I was puzzled to find that almost all cookbooks, whether general or devoted to game cookery, implied that the meat itself was indifferent, and palatable only after long hanging followed by prolonged soaking in a marinade of some sort. Of course there is bad luck as well as good in hunting, and hunters do find themselves with tough meat on their hands. My own experience, and that of my deer-hunting friends, indicates that one may expect the venison to be not inferior to beef in eating quality. I suspect that the tradition of disguising the flavor of venison with spices and herbs dates from the practices of Medieval times, and was originally dictated by necessity since a good deal of the meat must have been "high" to say the least. But we no longer present nosegays to the judge against the noisome smells of the courtroom, and we need not carry on an unnecessary convention and insist upon preparing our venison with a battery of spices, herbs and sauces. The main thing to remember is that venison is good eating: don't apologize for it.

It was my original intention to confine myself to the cutting up, freezing and cooking of deer meat, but so many people asked for practical directions on dealing with the preliminaries — that is, the most effective and least wasteful place to shoot the animal, as well as how to woods-dress it after shooting — that I co-opted a friend who is a fine hunter and a man of science as well, Frederick J. Turner, Professor of Forestry at Marlboro College. The gory details as well as all references to the United States Marines can, therefore, be attributed to him.

My thanks go, too, to L. David Hakey of Brattleboro, and to other capable friends, who generously read the early chapters with an experienced and friendly eye.

CHAPTER II

So Now It's Venison

YOU'VE GOT YOUR DEER. With one workman-like, well-placed shot your elusive quarry is transformed into meat: on the hoof he was *deer,* there at your feet he is *venison.* And as venison he will continue out of the woods, into the freezer and onto your table.

Until now Nature was responsible for the condition of the animal, playing weather against feed and pitting both against the regional quality of the herd. From here on out it's your care to insure that the meat is good.

FIRST CATCH YOUR DEER

Actually, however, concern for your own venison began earlier. The famous old recipe for jugged hare starts, as everyone knows, with the admonition: "First catch your hare. . . ."

I make no pretense here to being an expert guide for hunters. Sportsmen's magazines are prodigal with tips and instruction on how to become a successful hunter. Much of the advice they give is excellent and I would suggest reading some. But I want to underline three things you may pick up from these sources, if you don't know them already, because they have direct bearing on the subject of venison: know your weapon, know your firing time and know your target.

KNOW YOUR WEAPON

Before you can approach the ideal of killing your game every time with the first shot, you must know your rifle (or shotgun, if you operate in a state which forbids rifles). What is its effective range? More important, what is *your* effective range? Can you hit a five-inch bull's-eye at one hundred yards nine times out of ten? If you can't, don't expect to kill a deer at a similar distance. Experiment; try several shots at different ranges to discover just what you and your weapon can accomplish.

And don't forget to try close-range shots while you're at it. If your gun shoots a low-velocity bullet and is zeroed in for two hundred yards it may overshoot completely at one hundred yards.

KNOW YOUR FIRING TIME

Our civilization is steeped in legends of men quick on the draw, men who — with casual aim — "could knock out a squirrel's eye at ninety feet." Don't be taken in by these legends. Such accuracy is only possible in the imagination of a Wild West author who can ignore facts. The best hunter I know says it takes him from five to ten seconds to get his rifle into position, line up his sights, take a breath and squeeze the trigger. He says that the important thing is to learn how fast you can shoot accurately — and then live by it. For the benefit of anyone who shoots inaccurately, or who is a victim of "buck fever," he recommends the ritual taught in the United States Marines, i.e., recite to yourself the directions for shooting, at the moment that you are following them:

> *Get into position.*
>
> *Take up your slack.*
>
> *Line up your sights.*
>
> *Take a deep breath and let it out halfway.*
>
> *Hold it and squeeze it off.*

A hunter using this method of shooting has time to examine his target carefully and is not likely to come in with Tom Lehrer's full bag of "two game wardens, seven hunters and a cow."

KNOW YOUR TARGET

The next thing is to learn where to aim. Living things in general are hard to kill: they wouldn't be alive otherwise. Big living things — deer, bear, human beings, wolves, etc. — are usually very hard to kill. You must not only hit the critter, you must hit him in the right spot. A poorly-placed shot can result in: (1) losing the animal, (2) causing a great deal of suffering, (3) spoiling a lot of good meat.

So where do you aim? There is a poem, written around 1350 by a poet-poacher of England, describing one of his deer-poaching exploits. It includes the following lines:

> *And I hallede to the hokes* and the herte smote*
> *And happened that I hitt hym be-hynde the left sholdire*
> *Dead as a dorenayle doun was he fallen.*

Please note that the well-placed shot behind the "left sholdire" was effective then — and it is just as effective today. Consensus seems to be that a deer hit in this region drops and doesn't get up again. Seen from the side of the deer it is about equal to a five-inch circle on a small animal (hundred pounds) and is perhaps twice that size on a two-hundred pounder. In either case it isn't very big.

A shot in the brain is perhaps even quicker than a heart shot, but a deer's brain is awfully small (his frequent success in outwitting hunters is more a reflection on the intelligence of the hunter than a compliment to the deer). Unless the head shot is from very close range I wouldn't advise trying it.

I have heard reports that a neck shot is quite effective. If the bullet severs the spinal cord or any of the large blood vessels in the neck it is sure to be quickly fatal.

* hokes — *hooks, i.e., the trigger of his crossbow.*

So far as I can determine, these three areas are the only vital spots which fill all the requirements — the need to be sure, quick and non-wasteful.

Any shot in the spine will disable a deer so that you can approach and dispatch it, but this is cruel and wastes a lot of good meat. A high-powered, mushrooming slug can ruin quite a few chops as it rips obliquely through the backbone.

Leg shots are to be avoided, since they don't always disable the animal completely, and if they lodge in the hindquarters they may ruin many fine steaks. A deer can travel a long way on three legs, and from all reports it can survive so wounded for several days if not longer. Also I have heard of hunters being severely injured by wounded deer. One was kicked in the jaw by a down, but still lively, animal, and he ate through a straw for a month.

It's always a good idea, incidentally, to make sure that your deer really *is* dead before going to work on the carcass. A lid reflex check — running the end of a branch across his eyes and watching for a reaction — is a worthwhile safety measure.

I did not include the viscera (guts) among the three ideal target areas of a deer because, although a shot to such an area is likely to be fatal, a gut shot may not kill the animal immediately and anyway it makes for an awfully messy job when it comes to hog-dressing. Some hunters I know feel that a shot in the paunch can be responsible for off-flavor. They all agree that a wound in the intestines is a very poor shot; and that aside from a poor shot's being less humane and more wasteful, a deer merely wounded becomes a sick deer in no time at all, and the fever from sickness will soon affect the quality of the meat.

So far I have not dealt with any weapon except rifles or guns. The techniques for bow hunting are rather different, but the places to aim at for a quick, clean kill with a bow are the same as for a rifle or shotgun.

One more admonition that will already have occurred to the prudent reader: know your state law, particularly as regards tagging. Follow the law of the state and, where it is required, tag the deer as soon as downed.

HOG-DRESSING THE KILL

One of my hunter friends, who boasted of twenty seasons and only three without a kill, confessed that the twentieth finally showed him up: it was the first time he had been unable to persuade someone else to woods-dress his deer. He tackled it shakily, and on the whole managed rather better than he had feared. His wife, however, complained bitterly that it had taken her hours to remove a vast quantity of hairs when she was preparing the meat for the table.

Hog-dressing — or, as it is sometimes called, rough-dressing, woods-dressing, field-dressing or just plain gutting — consists of cutting open the carcass of the deer you have just killed and removing the internal organs.

For this operation you have carried with you a knife with a three-inch blade. (Or have you? A youthful hunter carried a well-sharpened two-edged knife that he had appropriated while serving with the Marines. At least he carried it until the very day he brought down his first deer, a handsome 165-pounder. All he had with him was his sister's pearl-handled penknife whose blade was a dainty one inch long and dull to boot. He insists that it did the job adequately.)

STICKING

One of the first things some hunters feel obliged to do is to stab or slit the throat to bleed the carcass. This is called "sticking." Consensus among people who have experimented is that this process is entirely unnecessary, and, in certain instances, definitely detrimental.

To any who object to departing from such an old custom, I would like to point out that slitting the throat to bleed the carcass is a rite which dates back to our pagan ancestors who thought that blood was demanded by their exigent gods. To put it more bluntly, the idea that a deer must be "stuck" and bled is a superstition. If your bullet goes into the thorax or paunch, the deer bleeds internally, and a massive release of blood occurs in the business of hog-dressing. If the bullet has lodged elsewhere, the superfluous blood will also flow out during dressing.

There is also a prime disadvantage to bleeding the carcass: it takes time. If the weather is cold and your shot was well placed, this is not an immediately important factor. But if the weather is warm — or if you were so unfortunate as to make a gut shot — you should lose no time in getting the animal hog-dressed.

Moreover, sticking a deer "properly" requires an undersized broadsword to go deeply enough into the base of the throat. Long-bladed knives are awkward to handle, and, except for sticking, they are vastly inferior to the good knife with the three-inch blade that you have brought with you.

All this may sound like rank heresy. However, it is not an un-substantiated opinion. Butchers and meatcutters, as well as hunters, agree with me. Furthermore, there is a financial reason for not sticking. If you wish to have the head mounted your taxidermist will charge you about twice as much if the throat is slit.

The instructions for sticking a deer can be summed up in one word: *DON'T!*

INSIDE STORY

The first major task of hog-dressing is to remove the innards, known commonly as guts (less commonly as viscera), a job which ought to be done as soon as possible since they start to degenerate very rapidly. You needn't get frantic about it, though. I have known of deer which were dead over an hour in warmish weather before they were dressed, and which were none the worse. But you had best get the affair over with, so as to have it out of the way.

For the benefit of those who have never before gutted any-thing, the following information may be helpful.

The body of the deer (or any other mammal for that matter) can be thought of as consisting of two parts: a fore and an aft. You are built that way too, so a bit of poking on your own body will give you some idea of how a deer is constructed. The fore part (called the thorax) is the part of the body which is sur-rounded by ribs. It contains the heart and the lungs with their accessories (blood vessels, windpipes, etc.).

The thorax is separated from the aft section (called the ab-domen) by a thin, muscular membrane, the diaphragm. In the abdomen are the stomach, liver, intestines, kidneys, and a great many other glands, organs, and what have you, which are the in-nards-guts-viscera.

The thorax is completely enclosed by a bony cage made of the ribs, backbone, and breastbone. The abdomen, on the other hand, has no such protection except for the backbone. This

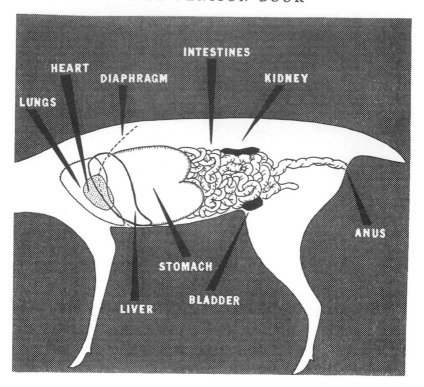

makes it very convenient when it comes to dressing the animal, since you don't have to chop through bones to open up the carcass via the abdomen.

Some hunters merely clean out the abdominal section, while others take out the heart and lungs as well. It is best to do both. If your shot was to the heart, the chest cavity is full of blood, which should be drained out immediately. Furthermore, the chest cavity should be opened to the air to allow the valuable meat along the back to cool off as rapidly as possible.

Cutting open the body and removing the innards doesn't require any superhuman skill or knowledge. Obviously, the thing to do is to slit the body and get the stuff out. Some authorities recommend that the opening be started from the aft end of the abdomen; others seem to prefer the forward end. I don't think it matters very much. For no special reason that he can think of, my chief expert always starts at the front and cuts back toward the tail.

Now that you know more or less where things are, put the deer on his back, roll up your sleeves and start cutting.

THE INITIAL CUT

Making the initial cut seems difficult if you don't know how. Don't try to cut into the body. The give and spring of the skin and hair make it hard to cut through without stabbing, and you'll probably end up by cutting into the stomach or doing something equally undesirable.

A much better way is to take, just aft of the breastbone, a pinch of skin between your thumb and forefinger, pull it away from the body (being careful not to slice your fingers in the process), and make a cut. If you happen to cut through the muscle wall underneath the skin at the same time, so much the better. If you don't, repeat the process until you are through into the gut cavity. You can always tell when you've penetrated the cavity because the muscle wall is quite hard, while everything underneath is quite soft and is gray in color.

OPENING THE ABDOMINAL CAVITY

As soon as you have made your first opening, stick two fingers under the muscle wall (palm outward and pointing to the rear of the deer, if you are starting from the forward end) and insert your knife between the two fingers under the wall with the sharp edge outward. Now start cutting. Be careful to keep the innards separate from the muscle wall so that your knife doesn't puncture them. Keep cutting right down the center line of the belly back to the hindquarters. When you get back as far as the hind legs, you will have a long slit out of which the intestines, etc., will be protruding. Soon you reach the end of the gut cavity and start hitting the meat of the hindquarters. That is all the opening you need, and so you end your cut into the cavity at this point.

But there are still a couple of things to do before trying to remove the innards. Holding the hind legs apart, continue your cut along the line of the crotch toward the tail, making this cut only skin deep. If you are dealing with a buck, cut the genitals off when you get to them. Keep going until you get to the anus. Now make a *deep* cut through the skin all around the anus.

To those who have never studied anatomy, I mention that the alimentary tract — i.e. the throat, esophagus or gullet, stomach and intestines both large and small — consists of what amounts to one long tube which is firmly attached in only two places: where it starts (at the mouth) and where it ends (at the anus). By making the deep incision around the anus you cut free one of the two attachments.

GUTTING

Now you can begin to remove things, starting at the bottom of the incision near the hindquarters. As I have said, the guts are not attached very firmly, so they will come out without much difficulty, particularly if the animal is now rolled over on his side, his feet downhill. There are a few minor places here and there where they are held by what is called mesentery tissue. This is rather thin, transparent, and not very strong. When you have removed enough of the intestine to make room for your hand, reach inside the cavity between the legs, take hold of the large intestine as near to the anus as possible, and pull it back through to the gut cavity and then out through the incision you have made in the abdominal wall. Now it is an easy matter to get the entire lower section of the alimentary tract out of the body intact (aside from any damage done in shooting the deer). Along with the alimentary tract will come most of the rest of the insides.

One step that may cause trouble is removing the bladder, the thin-walled, semi-transparent sac which, in every deer I have handled, was full of urine. Find the tube leading from it to the outside. Pinch the tube together with your fingers between the bladder and where you plan to make your cut to remove it; cut, and, using your grip on the tube, ease the bladder out with the rest of the lower gut.

When you have got this far, the worst part of the job is over, although you still have more work ahead. The alimentary tract is still attached to the fore section of the body. The easiest thing to do here is to cut the tube off *above* the stomach at the diaphragm, and remove the stomach and everything connected with it. This completes the cleaning of the gut cavity.

If you are a liver fancier you had better salvage the liver at this point. This is located roughly between the stomach, the diaphragm and the back. If you happen to be superstitious, you might try reading the future by the shape of the liver. I don't know what the signs are, but the Greeks and Romans were always at it. Make up your own signs and portents. They are just as likely to be right.

THE CHEST CAVITY

Next cut away the diaphragm. This is the thin wall of muscle which separates the chest cavity from the gut cavity. Reach in and pull out the heart and lungs and whatever else will come out. You may have to do some cutting here to sever the arteries (from the heart and the trachea or windpipes) which go up into the neck from the lungs.

CLEANING AND COOLING

When you are through, wipe out the inside of the entire cavity thoroughly with whatever is handy — a rag, your handkerchief, even a handful of clean grass. If you are near a brook it won't hurt to wash the cavity — and, if you made a gut shot, washing the cavity is a must: if there's no water handy, do it the first chance you get — and dry it thoroughly. (Contrary to popular belief this washing won't hurt anything. Commercial slaughter-houses use hot water and a brush, and scrub the cavity.)

The final step in hog-dressing will be to find a suitable stick to hold the body cavity open, so that the air can circulate through it. The purpose of this is to let the meat cool to prevent "souring." The body temperature of a deer is somewhere around 100 degrees Fahrenheit, which is an ideal temperature for bacteria to breed in; they can grow and multiply at an appallingly rapid rate, and sour your meat in no time. If you can't get the deer out of the woods immediately *don't leave it on the ground.* To promote the rapid cooling all meat should receive, hang the carcass in a tree, if you can manage to do so. Hang it by the head so any surplus blood can drain out.

CHAPTER III

But It's Still Not Steak

THERE ISN'T MUCH that is really comforting to be said about getting a deer back to civilization, once you've secured it. If it's a big one it will make a lot of hard work. If it's a little one it will merely mean less hard work. I once asked an experienced Vermonter for pointers on this problem. His reply wasn't very helpful: "Any way that gits him there is right."

OUT OF THE WOODS

The commonest way that I know of to get a buck out of the woods is to lay him on his back and drag him head first behind you, using the horns as handles. This takes two men and is not so easy as it sounds — and it doesn't apply at all to doe.

Many hunters carry a short length of ⅜-inch rope to use in dragging. Tie the head and forelegs together, put the other end of the rope over your shoulder, and start dragging. This is easier than dragging without a rope. Not much easier — just easier.

Another good method is to tie your line around the base of the horns (or around the neck if the horns won't provide a firm hold), then run it down the face between the eyes; take a half-hitch around the snout and tie the other end of the rope to a

short stick for one-handed dragging. This will tend to keep the head off the ground and clear of undergrowth.

Other methods that are used involve various carrying devices. One is an improvised stretcher carried by two men. It is made from two long poles, with a couple of crossbars tied between them, and the carcass rides on top — a sort of Chinese sedan-chair effect. Another is the one-man stretcher. This is the same as the two-man job, except that one man does all the work. You lash the deer to the stretcher, put one pole over each shoulder and get going, trailing the stretcher behind you. This is a slight improvement over trying to drag a heavy one by the horns yourself.

Another carrying method is to use a single pole. The deer's legs are tied together, the pole is slipped between its legs and the head is lashed to the pole. Two men carry this, one at either end, with the carcass swinging on the pole between them.

(One objection you may have to all this: where do you get the poles to make a stretcher? Good point. Where do you? Who always carries a hatchet while hunting? . . . But then, some very good hunters have never used a stretcher, either.)

I might mention that L. L. Bean of Freeport, Maine, advertises a single-wheel "toter." According to the testimonials he prints in his catalog, it is a very handy gadget. No hunter of my acquaintance has ever seen one used, so I cannot add any words on the subject.

When I was in grade school we had a story about Indians bringing in five deer to the first Pilgrim Thanksgiving. The illustrations showed the Indians carrying them on their backs, somewhat after the manner of fur neckpieces. They must have been awfully small deer or awfully big Indians. Anyway, I don't recommend trying it: carrying a deer out on your back is rather dangerous, aside from being difficult. There is a regrettable number of people in the woods during deer season who will shoot at anything resembling a deer (and even at things which

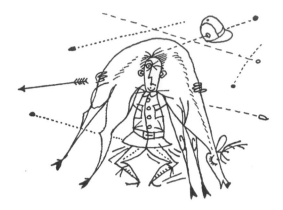

do not). Walking through the woods with a deer draped over your back is just asking for trouble.

While I'm on the subject of others in the woods, though, I would like to say that if you are hunting in a region where there are a great many hunters, you can usually find someone to help you get your kill out of the woods. I don't know whether there is a formal code of ethics on this subject or not, but I have been told by the finest hunters I know that a sportsman would always help another hunter get his deer out at no charge, and would expect the same favor for himself. If this isn't the accepted rule, it should be.

If worst comes to worst you can always skin the deer on the spot, quarter it and carry out the pieces — that is, if the laws of the state will allow it. Many states require you to bring in the animal, hog-dressed, to a weighing station, to provide statistics for Fish and Game Department records.

Perhaps the only painless way is to shoot your deer by the roadside so you don't have to drag it at all. Or, own a jeep that can be driven into the woods to pick up your animal. I have the jeep, but every time anyone in my orbit has shot a deer my jeep was either in the garage or doing the week-end shopping. So I've never had a hand in the painless method.

Once you have the deer out of the woods to a road there remains only the problem of getting it home. Here I warn you against the time-honored custom of tying the deer to the fender of your car and driving it triumphantly into town.

Don't put it next to the engine! It may look impressive, but it is the worst thing you can do to your venison. The heat of the engine will keep the carcass nice and warm — nice and warm for putrefying bacteria. Put it outside the car if possible, body cavity up, where the open air will reach it. If you have a luggage rack on top of your car tie the deer to it with its back to the car, the belly up. Or tie it to the rear bumper. But belly up, whatever you do. Yet, if for some reason you must place your kill over the front of the car, put blankets underneath the carcass to insulate it as much as possible from the engine's heat. This should be done only as a last resort. I don't recommend it.

N.B. Be sure that you are familiar with the game laws of the state in which you kill your deer. In some states it is forbidden to transport a wild deer carcass later than a specified time after the season is ended. Whether this law applies to an animal already butchered depends upon the circumstances, game wardens tell me. At any rate, a friend of mine bought a carcass from a hunter who had taken the deer legally, only to find that he could not get the animal home without breaking a state law. He took the risk, but he is a law-abiding man and he felt guilty about it for some time afterward. In addition, some killed game cannot be brought into some states without permission being obtained to import and possess it. These regulations are designed primarily to curb the activities of that bane of all good hunters, the poacher; still, it is best for all hunters to know the laws and to obey them in letter as well as in spirit.

TO HANG OR NOT TO HANG

The view that venison must always be hung — usually the time suggested is from two to three weeks — in order to make the meat tender and take away the gamy flavor, is nonsense.

I know that this statement will raise the hackles of many traditionalists. Herewith I shall defend it.

My first inkling that hanging is unnecessary came many hunting seasons ago when I had, in a family emergency, sole charge of a fine buck which had been killed and brought out of the woods one Saturday morning. By dawn of the following day, and for some time thereafter, not a soul would be on the premises to care for the venison. So we packed it into the freezer locker the same day, and the result, weeks later, was the best-flavored and most tender venison I had ever had a hand with.

I wanted to know why my defiance of tradition had brought a benefit, and not a punishment in the form of inferior meat; so I began scouting around among my friends. And I discovered that a surprising number of them had omitted hanging their deer. Once the carcass had cooled, they cut it up and ate it or stored it. Each of them assured me that such unhung venison was excellent — not a trace of gaminess, either.

Next, I stumbled upon a fact which I have taken into consideration ever since: if, for whatever reason, the carcass is hung for a prolonged period, the hide contributes to the gamy flavor many persons object to. If you don't believe me, taste a mouthful of hair from the next deer you get! If you leave the hide on for any length of time, the oil — or whatever it is which contains this disagreeable flavor — can diffuse through the skin into the meat. Yet, if you hang it for the traditionally proper time with the hide removed, the outside of the meat tends to turn black and unappetizing. So this gives me another argument against hanging — hide on or hide off.

But to me the most interesting and persuasive demonstration against the utility of prolonged hanging comes from the results of recent experiments with quick-freezing *versus* hanging.

At a meatcutters' institute held not long ago it was reported that (as the investigators had suspected before they began formal comparisons) quick-freezing as a means of tenderizing meat is equivalent to as many as 30 days' hanging under the best conditions.

There are a number of actual disadvantages to hanging.

If you do hang, the meat should be hung in a place which has a nearly-constant temperature, preferably not over 40 degrees Fahrenheit. Most homes are not equipped with such a room. Some cellars fit these conditions, but they are usually quite musty — a characteristic which transfers itself quickly to the meat. If you hang it outdoors, or even in a shed, you are at the mercy of weather changes: it may get too hot; or, strangely enough, it may get too cold. Even if you are an exponent of hanging, you should never hang a deer if the temperature is colder than 10 degrees above zero. The outside of the carcass quick-freezes, and some sort of thermal barrier is formed so that the innermost parts of the venison don't cool off. The result is spoilage.

Another disadvantage to hanging is that there are a great many creatures around who like venison. A friend shot a fine eight-pointer one year and, since the weather was cool, hung it in his garage. The next morning he went out and saw to his dismay what was left of his buck. A couple of neighborhood dogs had dropped in for a feast, and it was a total loss.

So by far the best thing to do is not to hang at all. Skin the carcass as soon as possible. If the venison has not yet cooled after this operation, hang it until it has: *and twelve to twenty-four hours should be sufficient.* But if the weather is hot and you have no way to cool the carcass, you had better start butchering right away.

I do concede that in some cases venison can be made more tender through aging, but there is no need at all to hang if you have access to a quick-freezer which will age the meat for you; and even if you can't quick-freeze the disadvantages of hanging outweigh the advantages.

There *are* minor benefits to hanging — respite and vanity. Hanging does give you a rest before you must get down to the business of butchering and processing. And vanity — well, vanity is human and I have my full share of it. But I would rather be vain of the results on my dinner table than take bows for a carcass strung up in my yard.

SKINNING

There is more than one way to skin a cat — so goes the old saying. It holds for deer, too. I have seen four or five different sets of directions for skinning deer, all differing in some respects. Here's the way I like to see it done.

As I mentioned before, you should skin the deer as soon as you can. Besides protecting flavor, early skinning makes your job simpler: the hide comes off more easily if the animal has not been dead too long.

At the start of the operation the deer should be lying on the ground on its back. Remember that in hog-dressing you have already slit the skin from the aft end of the gut cavity to the base of the tail. Begin now at right angles to this cut, making another cut through the skin, on the inside of each hind leg, starting at the crotch and running all the way down to the heel, continuing around the foot close to the heel. (Note here that what I have called the heel is called the knee by many people. Don't make their mistake. Deer, horses, cows and other hooved mammals walk on their toenails. Starting at the hoof and moving upward toward the body, the first straight section — vertical on the live, standing animal — is the foot; and the first joint is the heel — called the hock on horses — not the knee. It points backward on deer, as it does on you.)

All right. You have made the leg cuts. Now, straddling the carcass and facing its tail, start loosening the skin just aft of the opening you made when you gutted the animal — about where the hind leg joins the body. Except to begin the cut, very little knife work is necessary. Pull the skin away from the flesh far enough to allow you to put your hand inside the pocket you have created. Then work your hand under the skin around the hips toward the back. At the same time you are working toward the back, work your hands fore and aft along the flank and the outside of the hind leg, separating the skin from the flanks.

When you have loosened the skin about halfway around to the back, you can peel the hind legs, working toward the heel from the opening you have made. If the skin sticks to the flesh at any point, so you can't get your flat hand under it, you can probably get it loose by doubling your fist and twisting your wrist to pry it. Don't use a knife any more than you have to.

If you're worried about the scent glands (musk sacs) in the hind legs, they will come off with this skinning.

Possibly an easier method of skinning the hind legs is to start at the heel and peel the skin back toward the hips, rather than the other way around. I'm not recommending this procedure because you are likely to take off some of the flank meat by accident when you get down to that region. The rather more laborious method I have described above is the best one in the long run.

When you have the hind legs bare, hoist the deer into the air. Common practice is to make a slit between the Achilles tendon and the bone on each leg; thrust a stick about the diameter of a broom handle through the slits; tie a rope to the middle of the stick; throw the free end of the rope over a convenient branch or beam, and hoist away. But one time when I was helping to do all this I cut a tendon by mistake and found myself on the ground with a 165-pound deer carcass on top of me. Since then I have recommended a second method, and one that seems on the whole to be more satisfactory: tie one end of a long piece of rope around the leg just above one rear hoof, and the other end to the other leg above its rear hoof; throw the doubled rope over a branch; hoist, and make the loop fast. If the deer is hung this way one knot will hold the critter in the air if the other knot slips.

When the carcass is suspended head-down in the air the skin from the rear legs hangs down on each side. Now, working from behind the animal, pull the skin over and down the rump. The tail offers very little difficulty. Work the hide off to the base of the tail; then grab the end of the tail and pull. The hide should slip right off the tailbone. If it doesn't, cut off the tailbone.

Continue skinning down toward the head. Everything really goes quite easily. A steady downward pull will separate the skin from the flesh. Occasionally you may need to cut a bit of connecting tissue which refuses to separate from the skin, but otherwise use the knife very little.

The forelegs don't present any serious difficulty either. Peel the skin off as if you were taking off a pullover sweater, cutting it off at the wrists. Keep on skinning down to the base of the skull. Remove the head by cutting through the flesh at the base of the skull until you're into the neck bones, then twist the head until it separates from the neck. This completes the skinning job.

What to do with the skin is something of a problem. I have never discovered any way of home-curing hides satisfactorily. In most areas where there is much deer hunting there is usually someone who buys hides, paying one to two dollars a hide, according to its condition. If there is such a person near you, take your hide to him immediately and let him worry about salting and preserving it.

But if you can't do this you will have to take a few precautionary steps to save the hide. The fore-end of the skin is still in the shape of a pullover sweater, so you must now open it down the front to the head, then remove the head. Next, slit the skin along the inside of the front legs so the hide can be spread flat. Scrape all the meat and fat from the hide and put about two pounds of salt on the flesh side. After a week of such curing you can roll the hide and the skin will keep in good condition until you can dispose of it one way or another.

If you have a handsome head and wish to have it mounted, the best thing to do is to take the entire head and hide off to a taxidermist immediately and let him carry on from there.

However, if some time is going to elapse before you can get your trophy to the taxidermist, cut the skin at the shoulders and scrape off what flesh you can, salting the inside of the hide liberally. Be sure to leave plenty of neck and shoulder hide, called the "cape." A safe rule is to leave on from six to eight inches more hide than you think is necessary. Skinning the head is a ticklish process, and I wouldn't advise you to try it on a real prize. On the whole it's easier and cheaper — sentiment aside — to pick up a mounted head at an auction.

If you have a deer with a fine rack of horns, you can save the horns for a trophy by sawing off the top of the skull so as to include both antlers. Place the skull section of the horns into boiling water for an hour or so; clean off any hide or tissue which may still be adhering to it, then dry it.

CHAPTER IV

The Kitchen a Shambles

AT SOME TIME or other you have probably described your own kitchen as "a complete shambles." But when you cut up and package your venison at home you will be speaking the literal truth: "*Shambles: a butcher's slaughter-house*" (OXFORD DICTIONARY).

For the butchering, or cutting-up operation, you will need three tools — a *sharp* butcher knife, a meat cleaver or sharp hatchet, and a saw. (I have used both a meat-saw and a back-saw, and have found them both satisfactory.)

HALVING THE CARCASS

• The first task in this operation is to split the carcass in half lengthwise. Hang the carcass head down and, with the cleaver or hatchet, split the breastbone from the belly to the neck.

> If you want two circular neck roasts — with the bone running through the middle, handier for cooking — the neck should be cut off before the carcass is halved.

• Then split the pelvis (or H-bone) in half down the middle. This leaves the carcass completely open on the belly (or ventral) side from the tail to the neck.

• Complete the halving job by sawing down through the backbone from tail to neck.

> This feat is sometimes difficult. Your aim is to split the backbone exactly in the middle. As with many other things, you will find that the desire outruns the performance. The easiest way, I've found, is to work from the belly side — i.e., with the back away from you and the open body cavity toward you. This position enables you to see (sort of) what you are doing. Inside the body cavity you can make out the outline of the backbone and you can guide your saw accordingly. You can check progress by observing whether you are splitting the spinal cord (the long white cord, the diameter of your little finger, which runs down the middle of the backbone). I *have* used a hatchet for this job; but it is rather more messy, although considerably quicker, than using the saw.

• When this splitting operation is completed you can take down the halves of the carcass and carry them to your butchering table.

> A sturdy table with a clean wooden top that you don't mind scratching is ideal to work on; but I have done my butchering on a rickety, linoleum-topped affair which bid fair to collapse under every blow of the cleaver.

• If you haven't already cut off the feet, do so now. This is accomplished by cutting the tendons around the wrist and ankle joints, then working the feet back and forth smartly, until they snap off.

QUARTERING THE CARCASS

The next step requires you to cut each half into three sections. For some reason this step is called "quartering."

• Take one of the halves. Remove the hindquarter by making a

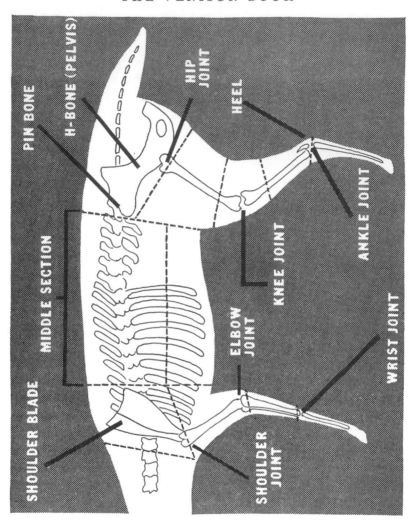

cut *just forward* of the pin-bone (this is the name for the front part of the pelvis).

• Free the forequarter by making another cut *just to the rear* of the rearmost part of the shoulder blade.

This cut is made five (sometimes six) ribs back from the neck.

- Treat the second half of the carcass in the same manner.

    When you have separated each half according to these directions, you will have six pieces comprising two middle sections, two forequarters and two hindquarters.

1.   CUTTING UP THE MIDDLE SECTION

- Remove the flank from the lower, or belly, part of the middle section.

    This cut is made at the point where the meat thins out, about halfway down the middle section. The flank doesn't amount to much on a deer. I trim off any fat and put the meat aside for stew. Some people put this meat into hamburger (or deerburger, if you're a purist).

    The upper, or backbone, part of the middle section is usually made into chops (or roasts if you prefer), thus:

- On the front half of the middle section — this front portion is called the saddle, and it is where the ribs are — slice down between the ribs until you reach the backbone. Then complete each cut with a sharp blow with your cleaver.

    This cleaver blow is tricky for a beginner because it is necessary to hit both hard and accurately. With a little practice you'll get the knack of it. RIB CHOPS result from this operation.

- On the rear part of the middle section — this portion is the loin, and there are *no ribs* here — slice down to the bone in the same manner, then use your cleaver.

    Here your cut will be guided by the vertebrae, or small projections from the backbone. You have LOIN CHOPS when you're finished.

N.B.   In these directions for cutting up the saddle and loin I have mentioned only chops. But if you want roasts — and your deer must be a large one to make roasts worth-while — you merely leave a certain number of rib chops intact, or a certain length of loin intact.

2. CUTTING THE FOREQUARTER

The forward section, which includes the front leg, is cut into ROASTS and STEW MEAT. Do it this way:

- Cut off the front leg *just below* the shoulder joint.
- Cut off the neck in front of the shoulder blade.

    The neck can make a roast, or go into stew or mincemeat. If the deer is a large one, the shoulder section, or chuck, can be made into two roasts. You do this by cutting down through the shoulder blade and backbone at a right angle to the backbone. If you don't like bony carving, though, it might be a good idea to bone the shoulder roast and so get rid of the shoulder blade and the inconvenient ridge running down the middle of it. (And stuffing goes mighty well with a boned shoulder roast.)

- Cut off the lower part of the leg just above the elbow joint.

    The upper part makes a leg roast. What is left — the lower part, or shank — can go into stew.

3. CUTTING THE HINDQUARTER

- Cut off the leg just below the hip joint.

    The hip joint is deeply buried and rather hard to find, but with a bit of prodding and poking you will locate it. This cut will follow and be guided by two small projections from the lower part of the pelvis bone; the cut calls for a long sharp knife, and for the saw when you come to the bone. The top part of this big piece you have just severed makes an excellent RUMP ROAST. If the deer is a large one, this part can be made into two roasts. To make this cut, slice *in front* of the hip joint at a right angle to the backbone. You'll need your saw, of course.

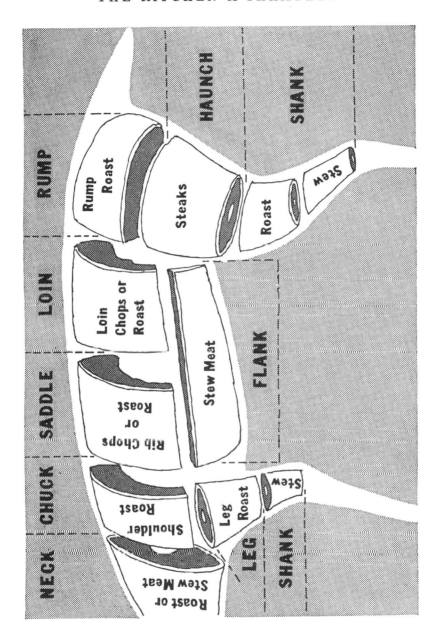

• Start slicing Steaks from the large end of the leg (the haunch) until they get too small for what your idea of a steak should be.

Remember that these steaks are considered by many to be the great venison delicacy, and they should be cut to be worthy of their reputation. Be sure to leave enough meat intact at the smaller end of this section to give you a decent-sized roast.

• Cut off your Leg Roast about one third of the way down the leg from the knee joint.

The balance of the leg (the shank) can go into stew meat.

OR DO IT THIS WAY

The procedure I have just described for cutting up the carcass is the one generally recommended. Here is another method, one which I prefer because there are fewer bones to carve around. It is perhaps a little trickier to follow, however.

• Halve the carcass in the manner given above.

• Then, pulling each leg assembly out from the middle section — much as you do in carving a wing or a thigh from a turkey — cut off each leg assembly.

You will notice in the illustration on page 34 that neither the fore- nor the hind-leg bone is connected directly to the backbone. They are fastened only loosely in each case, a fact which (although it seems a rather flimsy way to put a critter together) makes a deer convenient to cut up. In the case of the foreleg, the cut is between the shoulder blade and the ribs. In the case of the hind leg, it is between the pelvis and the backbone.

• Cut up the fore- and hindquarters as described on page 36.

The front-leg assembly should yield two roasts: a Shoulder Roast which includes the shoulder blade and the shoulder joint; and a LEG ROAST which goes from just below the shoulder joint to below the elbow joint.

• Cut up the middle section, starting from the tail and working to the front. Cut off a ROAST, then LOIN CHOPS and RIB CHOPS until they get too small; follow along with a SHOULDER ROAST and, finally, cut a NECK ROAST.

ODDS AND ENDS

You have completed the butchering operation. There are, of course, other variations which you can follow according to your preferences and depending upon the size of your deer. If you have a small deer and a large company to feed, you may prefer to serve up an entire leg assembly as a roast. Or, if your deer is large, and you are feeding only a few people, you may want to cut as many steaks and chops as you can get.

One more thing concerning butchering. How much meat can you get from a deer? This depends upon the size and condition of the animal. Generally speaking, the larger the deer the more meat you will get in proportion to the rough-dressed weight. From one large buck, weighing 156 pounds hog-dressed, we got the following yield:

ROASTS	40 pounds
STEAKS	21 pounds
CHOPS	21 pounds
NECK ROAST	10 pounds
STEW MEAT and HAMBURGER	24 pounds
HEART and LIVER	5 pounds

A total of 121 pounds of meat. The yield was approximately three-quarters of the dressed weight.

From a smaller deer, weighing 90 pounds, the yield was between 40 and 45 pounds of meat — scarcely one half the dressed weight.

I want to make a point right now, in behalf of venison. A great deal of the downright dislike of venison for its own sake is caused by the treatment it receives. If venison were handled with the care given beef — if it were not shot several times, not dragged over the ground, not shipped unrefrigerated on the hood of an automobile — it would taste better. Most venison, if it were beef, would never pass government inspection.

So you should take especial pains with your venison during this whole butchering operation. There will be traces of clotted blood, hairs and bits of bone to deal with, no matter how careful you have been in dressing and transporting your deer. Before you package your meat for the freezer — or process it in other ways — wipe the pieces with a cloth wrung out in water to which you have added a little vinegar. Doing this will pick up most of the hairs, etc.; and ordinary tweezers are useful for extracting any bone chips or hair which escape the cloth.

I assume that you will want to keep the "variety meats" — the liver (unless you have already celebrated your kill by eating it), the heart, kidneys and perhaps the brains. If you don't use them right away they should be frozen.

Some people make hamburger from the scraps that are too small or too torn to chunk for stew meat; or, at this stage of the game, some are so tired that even stew meat goes into hamburger. To make hamburger, add one third as much beef fat (suet) as you have venison and grind the two together. (My regular butcher always does this for me.)

For venison sausage, add one third as much fresh fat pork as you have venison and grind the combination. To four pounds of ground meat you may add:

5 teaspoons salt	1 teaspoon sugar
2 teaspoons freshly-ground pepper	4 teaspoons sage
½ teaspoon ground cloves (or nutmeg)	

You may prefer to omit the sage, or part of it, because it is so strongly flavored, or to use other combinations of spices.

CHAPTER V

Keep It Yourself

IT'S ALWAYS PLEASANT to give something to people if they like it as much as you do, and this holds true for presents of venison. Yet it's no fun at all — and wasteful into the bargain — to give away out of desperation good meat you could use yourself. Today you can enjoy all of your deer, thanks to home freezers, commercial lockers and good canning techniques and equipment. And when you do give venison to your friends they are receiving a welcome treat, not doing you a favor by taking it off your hands.

PACKAGING FOR THE FREEZER

At present freezing seems to be the ideal way to store surplus food. It has not only entirely changed the methods of preserving fresh meat and made-dishes, it has given us a high standard of palatability.

If you have no deep-freezer of your own you can rent space from your neighborhood freezer locker at a moderate cost; and its charge for cutting up and packaging deer meat is presently about eight cents a pound.

But if you have butchered your deer yourself you will certainly want to package the meat yourself. It is logical to wrap your venison for the freezer immediately after you cut it up, or you can package it as you go along. The materials you should have on hand are: plenty of the heavy wrapping paper recommended for use in quick-freezing meats; aluminum foil (if you do not mind the expense); freezer tape to seal the packages; plastic bags to hold hamburger, sausage, etc., and a good grease pencil suitable for marking grease-proof paper.

I have found that the heavy wrapping paper made expressly for freezer use is the most satisfactory material for packaging my meat. The bones in venison are sharp and are likely to puncture the pliofilm type of wrapping, destroying the seal. If air reaches the meat the surface will become dry (so-called freezer burn), a condition which spoils both the looks and the quality of the meat. Two layers of paper, the outside layer sealed with tape, will do a workmanlike job. Wrap the first layer of paper closely about the meat to exclude air, and don't stint the size of your paper; wrap the second layer to cover the seams in the first layer, and seal it with tape. A very satisfactory wrapping consists of a layer of aluminum foil pressed closely around the meat to exclude the air and an outer layer of freezer paper sealed with tape.

You should mark your packages as you go along, using your grease-proof pencil (or ordinary crayon if your pencil has got lost in the confusion) to describe the contents. I begin by marking simply: *Venison, 1957, 6 chops*, etc. But I soon find myself becoming more specific: *Venison, 6 chops (rather small)*, or *Venison steak, 2 pounds (not for guests)*. You will know exactly what you have if you write *Venison roast, 4 pounds (bony)* or *Venison stewmeat (bits and pieces)*.

This explicitness is one of the advantages of packaging your venison yourself. Be careful to package the meat in amounts that you normally use (or tell the locker man to do so, if he is handling your deer for you). Be conservative in your estimates. You can always take out an extra package for additional guests, but if you have thawed more meat than you need for just your family you are committed to cooking it at once.

PRESSURE CANNING

Pressure canning is a great deal more work than packaging your venison for storage in the freezer. Canning also greatly reduces the versatility of your venison: the meat must be cut into pieces small enough to go into a jar or a can and, since proper canning means the equivalent of long boiling, all your meat has the texture of pot roast or stew. Perhaps the greatest disadvantage to canning meats in the past has been the inability to insure reasonable safety, to prevent spoilage that could occur, undetected, and so allow dangerous bacteria to develop in the canned product.

However, it is only fair to point out that with the introduction of the *pressure canner* meat can be properly preserved. If you follow the manufacturer's directions to the letter you can feel confident that the meat will be safe to use.

If, for reasons of your own, you do wish to preserve your venison by canning, there are some important *do's* and *don'ts*.

DON'T ATTEMPT TO CAN MEAT *(packed in jars or cans either raw or cooked)* UNLESS YOU ARE USING A PRESSURE CANNER. The hot-water bath, which is safe for acid fruits or tomatoes, is quite inadequate to cope safely with protein products. Use TIN CANS which can be sealed in the same manner commercially-treated products are sealed, and follow the manufacturer's directions faithfully. Cans involve considerable expense for a hand-sealer, but they are satisfactory.

Be quite certain that you have understood and have followed the directions that come with your pressure canner, as well as the directions for sealing the containers you are using.

You must observe scrupulous cleanliness while processing meat, so that the utensils used, as well as the meat itself, cannot become contaminated before sealing.

All cans should be tested after processing and any can which shows the slightest hint of imperfect sealing must be rejected. Before using canned products you should make certain that no spoilage has occurred during storage. Do NOT TASTE any canned product if you are suspicious. THROW IT AWAY IMMEDIATELY.

Check the pressure gauge on your canner; it may not be registering the correct amount of pressure. Adjust the gauge or compensate during your canning process for any variation you have discovered.

With these reservations and recommendations in mind, here are the general directions for canning venison.

There are two methods of packing meat in containers prior to the pressure canning process: meat may be packed partially cooked and still hot, or it may be packed raw. The pressure canning process is the same for either packing method, both of which are given below.

Before you start to can, be sure that you have all the utensils you will need at hand and that they are scrupulously clean. Read the manufacturers' directions for pressure canner and jars or can-sealer (if you are using tin cans), and be sure that you understand how the mechanisms work. You are going to have to work fast. It is disastrous to have to experiment when you have a quantity of meat waiting to be processed.

If you are using glass jars with rubber rings and lids, be sure that the rings are new and the jars and lids are not cracked or chipped. Wash the jars and lids in hot soapy water and rinse them thoroughly. Boil the rings for ten minutes. Read the maker's directions for sealing.

Use tin cans if possible and choose those recommended by the manufacturer for canning meat. Some cans are enamel-lined; some have paper gaskets. There are several sizes of cans: a No. 2 can holds 2½ cups (20 ounces), a No. 2½ can holds 3½ cups (28 ounces) and a No. 3 can holds 4 cups (32 ounces).

Test your can-sealing equipment by half-filling a can with water and sealing it. Then immerse the can in water for a few minutes: if any air bubbles rise, the sealer is not working properly and must be corrected according to the maker's directions.

If your cooker has a weighted gauge it will be properly adjusted provided that it is clean and unclogged. Check your dial gauge at least once at the start of the canning season.

Meat is processed at 10 pounds pressure (240 degrees Fahrenheit at sea level). To correct the pressure for altitude, add *1 pound* pressure for each 2,000 feet above sea level, and process for the time specified.

Meat to be canned should be in perfect condition. The meat should be chilled for at least 24 hours to get rid of all animal heat. Large pieces of meat must be boned and cut to fit the jars or cans; small pieces and scraps of clear meat can be canned for stews. As a guide, 4½ to 5½ pounds of venison *at untrimmed weight* will be required to fill either a quart jar or a No. 3 can. In cutting meat to fit the container, cut so that the grain will run lengthwise of the container.

Hot-Pack Method. Put the meat into a large pan or kettle with enough water to keep it from sticking to the pan as it cooks. Cover and cook slowly until the meat is about half-cooked. Turn the pieces once or twice so all the meat will cook evenly. Pack the hot meat into the containers, leaving *1 inch* at the top for glass jars, ½ inch for cans. You may add salt or not as you like. If you wish to add salt, 1 teaspoon should be added to quart jars or No. 3 cans, ¾ teaspoon to No. 2½ cans, ½ teaspoon to pint jars or No. 2 cans. Cover the meat with the hot meat juice, adding boiling water or stock if needed. Leave *1 inch* of space at the top of jars; fill cans to the top. Remove air bubbles with the blade of a knife. Adjust the lids on jars; "exhaust" and seal tin cans. Process at 10 pounds pressure for 75 minutes for pint jars or No. 2 cans. Quart jars, No. 2½ cans and No. 3 cans should be processed for 90 minutes.

Raw-Pack Method. Pack the raw meat into the containers, adding salt if you wish. The jars or cans should be filled nearly to the top. Put the containers into a large, deep pan with a cover and fill the pan with water to within a couple of inches of the tops of the jars or cans. Cover the pan and, after the water is boiling gently, cook for 1 hour if you are using cans, for 1¼ hours with glass jars. A thermometer inserted in the middle of the contents of each container should register 170 degrees Fahrenheit.

Push the meat well down into the cans or jars and top the meat with boiling water or stock as in the hot pack. Adjust lids on jars or seal cans; process in the pressure canner as described in the hot-pack method.

When the pressure processing is completed, reduce the pressure in the canner *slowly* — especially if you are using glass jars — to avoid breakage. After the pressure is reduced, allow 15 to 20 minutes before taking the jars out of the canner. Finish sealing the jars if they are not self-sealing. Place the hot jars on a dry, folded cloth out of the way of drafts. Do not let jars touch. If you use cans, the cans may be removed as soon as processing is finished and pressure has been allowed to escape by gently easing the gauge or opening the petcock. Cool the cans in cold water and allow air to circulate around them.

When the jars are cool they should be examined. If you find a jar whose seal leaks, you can, of course, use the contents immediately; or the meat may be reprocessed in another jar. The containers should be labelled with the date as well as with a full description of the contents. Store canned foods in a cool, dark, dry place. Before using, carefully examine each jar or can, and if there is any bulging or leakage *discard the contents.* To be quite safe, home-canned meat is boiled by many people for 15 to 20 minutes before it is eaten.

You may can stews, soups, or gravies, meatballs, etc., using your usual recipes and following the procedures outlined. Do not season your meat too highly before you can it. It is better to add herbs with strong flavors, like sage or oregano, when the meat is opened for serving.

CURING WITH SALT AND SMOKE

I must admit that I don't know from my own experience much about pickling or smoking meat. I do know that it is considerably less of a chore than it used to be, since there are now "meat guns" or syringes that force the curing fluid into the meat, thus obviating the necessity for soaking it in brine. There are also smoke-treated salts, and even liquids, with an old-fashioned smoke flavor. These are rubbed into, or painted onto, the chunks of meat after they have been treated with the salting gun. Detailed directions come with the equipment.

Pickling in brine or salt-curing, followed by smoking in a smokehouse, call for a good deal of experience as well as the necessary barrels, fuel, smokehouse, etc. — and, I should imagine, a good deal of energy and enthusiasm into the bargain. I shall not pretend to offer advice where I cannot speak with authority, so I suggest that you consult your local freezer locker experts: they usually carry for sale the salt and equipment necessary and are kind about giving advice. They also do an excellent job of curing meat at a very nominal cost.

Jerked venison, or "jerky" — that is, thin strips of venison salted and dried in the sun, even smoked if you like — is still mentioned by some old-time hunters with a certain nostalgia. I doubt if many people would bother with it today. But perhaps you regard it as a delicacy or as a romantic legacy from Ernest Thompson Seton days. (This is the more likely if you have not tasted it, but have only read about it in adventure books.) If you would like to experiment with it, this is the general idea.

You can use any cut of meat to make "jerky." If you are just trying it on for size, though, you won't be wasting superior meat if you cut your strips from the flank.

Cut the meat *with the grain* into strips 1 inch wide and ½-inch thick. Make them any length you can. Prepare a brine of 6 quarts of water to 2 pounds of salt (the brine should be salty enough to float an egg in its shell). Soak the strips for 2 days in the brine. Remove and wipe dry. Hang the strips of meat in the sun to dry; they may be pinned to the clothesline with spring clips. When they are dry they may be smoked or simply stored as is, in an airy place well protected with netting.

CHAPTER VI

Venison Recipes

S O F A R I have not recommended anything about camp cookery, and I am not going to do so now. The equipment and location of the hunting camp and the organization of a camping holiday are highly personal matters, and each camper has traditions of his own as to if, when and how he serves venison in camp.

Later on I shall speak of some simple ways to treat liver and kidneys, etc., and if camp cooks agree with them I shall be gratified — and not chagrined in the least if they don't. For the benefit of those people who feel that venison is unworthy unless it is spiced beyond recognition I say that often venison cooked in camp is excellent: it has been treated as a meat good in its own right, as indeed it is.

Beyond this I shall not go. In my experience campers tend to be suspicious if not actually contemptuous of any methods but their own — and I don't want to find myself in anyone's black books!

SEASON TO TASTE

I suspect that the present fashion for using a variety of herbs in meat cookery has gone too far, and as a result nearly everything tastes like everything else.

Adding thyme, basil, marjoram, oregano, generous pinches of this-and-that has now become standard operating procedure in all "made dishes." In particular, oregano (which is the Italian name for wild marjoram) and thyme are strong, individual flavors and can blanket other seasonings and obscure the original flavor of the meat ingredient. Some Italian recipes, like that for pizza, should include oregano. It is the taste one expects to find. However, to insist upon oregano in every stew, stuffing and sauce is to introduce a disastrous monotony, and the hand that rocks the cradle might exercise a bit of restraint. Another in this category is sage, traditional in stuffing for roast goose but possessing a flavor that one very soon tires of. Goose appears infrequently on most tables; the sage does very well on these occasions.

Along with too many herbs I deplore the use of too many spices. Uncounted recipes which call for such seasoning reflect, to my mind, historic techniques for coping with meat that has "gone by" or imply apologies for what should be regarded as a delicacy. Therefore I have included spices only where the characteristic of a dish requires them. Once more, of course, the decision rests with you. Nutmeg, cinnamon and cloves are the additions noticed most often. N.B. Most people loathe caraway seeds!

Salt, freshly-ground pepper, monosodium glutamate — sugar, if you are using tomatoes — these blend with, but do not disguise, the original savors. Vegetable flavors — onions and/or garlic, chopped parsley and celery — are complementary and bring out the taste of the meat. They are a must for gravies, court bouillon and many sauces.

For gentle variation I do recommend currant jelly put right into the sauce in which the meat is cooked, since this bright-tasting jelly so rightly accompanies venison roasted or broiled. Wine, too, is a matter of taste — and virtually a subject by itself. Sometimes I use dry vermouth instead of sherry; the result is pleasant and subtle and not quite so sweet as sherry.

MARINADES

A disproportionate number of venison recipes begin by ordering a prolonged bath in a marinade rather in the manner of the Victorian doctor who set great store by "hot fomentations" as a precautionary measure.

Some writers explain this preliminary, almost therapeutic, soaking on the grounds that without it the meat is either tough or gamy or both. Marinating may succeed in partially disguising the toughness of the meat, although I doubt if it helps any real problem. Long, slow cooking, or pressure-pan cooking, will usually take care of the less choice cuts of meat. The so-called gamy flavor, if and when it exists, comes from the fat. If most of the fat is removed when the meat is prepared for freezing or cooking, and strips of bacon or lardoons substituted when the meat is cooked, there will be no need to drown the venison in a witch's brew. The marinade now remains as a preliminary to certain dishes: Sauerbraten, for instance, is always marinated before cooking, and the flavor of the marinade gives the Sauerbraten the tangy, spicy flavor we associate with it.

There are numberless combinations of wine, vinegar, lemon juice, water and spices which are labelled "marinade." Here are some samples. You can work out your own variations, adding or subtracting particular and distinctive flavors according to your preferences.

Marinade I

2½ cups red wine	10 whole cloves
1½ cups vinegar (*tarragon if you like*)	4 or 5 juniper berries
	1 large onion, peeled and
1 teaspoon salt	sliced thin
1 teaspoon dry mustard	2 cloves of garlic
2 bay leaves	1 tablespoon chopped celery
10 peppercorns (*black, unground*)	(*or celery seed*)

Put the piece of venison into an enameled, earthenware or stainless steel bowl or pan and pour over it the marinade. Cover with cheesecloth or a towel and let stand at least 24 hours — or up to

4 days — at a cool, but not refrigerated, temperature. The meat should be turned in the marinade so that the marinade reaches all parts of it. (The marinade need come only halfway up the meat if it is turned faithfully.) The meat is then cooked in the liquid or the meat may be roasted and the marinade used in making the gravy.

A couple of less elaborate mixtures to show you how cooks vary in their recommendations are:

Marinade II

1 cup olive oil   ½ cup lemon juice or vinegar

Pour over the meat and let stand for 24 hours, turning the meat in the mixture several times during the day. (This one seems to me to be too bland and flavorless, but it has been warmly recommended to me by friends, and it might be your choice.)

Marinade III

This one is simply a mixture of red wine and water — 2/3 wine to 1/3 water — with spices to taste.

Marinade IV

Vinegar (wine or cider vinegar) diluted with an equal amount of boiling water. One large onion, thinly sliced, and spices to taste.

Marinade V

In this marinade the onions are sautéed slowly in butter or olive oil until golden and transparent: don't let the onion get brown. When the onion is done add the following:

½ teaspoon celery seed, peppercorns, whole cloves. Generous pinches of thyme, basil, marjoram, rosemary, paprika, dill, grated horseradish. Any of the spices may be omitted without materially affecting the marinade.

In short, there are as many recipes for marinades as for martinis — and their adherents are as fanatical. If money and alcohol are no object, there is an excellent, and different, marinade. It is simple, too. A fifth of applejack plus 2 tablespoons Worcestershire sauce: highly recommended.

BROILING AND ROASTING

Steaks and Chops

The choicest and tenderest cuts of venison are the chops and steaks. Venison chops correspond to the rib roast in beef; steaks of course may be many and various. The cooking methods to be followed are the same as those you would use in cooking similar pieces of beef — broiling with or without charcoal, pan-broiling — whatever you think is the one and only way to deal with a steak or chop to bring it to perfection.

Here again it is advised that the fat (if any) should be trimmed from the meat before broiling. The meat may be brushed with olive oil, or butter may be rubbed into it, to counteract any tendency to dryness that may result from removing the natural fat. Chops may be neatly trimmed and a slice of bacon wrapped around each and fastened with a toothpick or skewer. If you pan-broil — a method I am leery of because it can come dangerously close to frying, and to my mind frying is a ruinous way to cook this meat — merely put 1 tablespoon of olive oil in the bottom of the pan to keep the meat from sticking.

As for salt, I always wait until the broiling is done to use it. Cooks are divided into two camps: (1) don't salt in the beginning because the juices will be drawn out and (2) season first because salting doesn't make much difference. Because of my allegiance to the salt-at-the-end camp, I wouldn't use salt in the pan to prevent sticking if I *did* pan-broil. Anyway properly trimmed venison has virtually no fat of its own and would be likely to stick in pan-broiling, regardless of salt.

Happy is the family that can agree on the "doneness" of its steak. It is almost impossible to do justice to the meat if you must take into consideration several opinions on the relative merits of "rare" and "well-done."

With venison even more than with beefsteak, the less the steak is cooked the juicier and more delicious it will be. But that is my opinion, and it must be admitted that there are many people who can't eat "underdone" meat of any kind; and for them further cooking is a necessity, else they will leave the meat untouched on the plate and very likely make remarks about it into the bargain. If there's a chance of such a calamity (which can utterly ruin a pleasant dinner), it is wise to serve chops rather than a large steak. Chops can be treated individually and each diner may have his cooked to his taste.

Do not ruin these superior cuts of meat by adding unnecessary gravies of any sort; save sauces for the less choice parts of the animal. Steaks and chops may be served *au naturel* with a lump of butter on top, or with a flavored butter if you prefer it. A few of these butters are described below, and you may wish to evolve specialties of your own.

Worcestershire sauce cannot legitimately be refused if demanded, and probably a thick sauce such as A–1 could be allowed as well. But *hide* the chili sauce and catsup: they don't belong in this company!

FLAVORED BUTTERS

Enough butter should be used to allow each serving to be about 1 teaspoonful. The proportions of flavoring to butter are not hard and fast — 1 tablespoon flavoring to ¼ pound of butter is

about right. The butter must be left at room temperature long
enough to soften until it can be easily worked. It must never be
melted to hasten the process! Work the flavoring into the butter
with a fork. After adding the flavoring the butter should be
thoroughly chilled in the refrigerator. Put a teaspoon of butter
on each chop, or spread evenly over the steak *immediately* before serving.

Parsley Butter

Fresh parsley chopped as fine as possible and added to the softened butter.

Chive or Watercress Butter

Use finely-chopped chives or watercress in place of parsley.

Anchovy Butter

Either anchovy filets or anchovy paste (which comes in a tube)
may be used. Pound and mash the filets or squeeze out 1 tablespoon of anchovy paste. Less salt will be needed in seasoning
the meat because the anchovy paste is salty.

ROASTS

A fine roast of venison should be served with pride if it has been
handled with respect. Treat your roasts as if they were compara-
ble cuts of beef, remembering only that you must compensate
for venison's having a great deal less fat. For my part, I'll assume that you *like* venison, and would no more marinate your
best roast than you would so soak and season a standing rib
roast of beef.

Whether you salt first or salt last; cook on a spit in a rotisserie;
in either a hot or a slow oven; on a rack; with foil or without it;
with your meat thermometer registering "rare" or "well-done"
— you have your own method.

And because it's unnecessary here to list all the kinds of beef
roasts and instructions for cooking them — substituting "veni-

son" for "beef" — I give only two recipes in this section. One is unusual in its goodness and its simplicity and is a favorite; the other describes a stuffing you could also find useful in, say, a rolled shoulder roast.

Gespickter Rehfleisch

In plain English, this is a larded venison roast and it is an excellent way of using the neck. You will have two neck roasts (unless you cut the neck into pieces for stew); try this recipe for one of them. It is vouched for by a wonderful cook I know from Germany. She swears by the tenderizing effect of marinating the meat overnight in buttermilk.

neck roast	bacon for larding
buttermilk for marinating	salt and pepper

Marinate the meat overnight in buttermilk. After removing the meat from the buttermilk, wipe it off with a clean towel and put it into a roasting pan. Lard with strips of bacon, threaded into a larding needle. The lardoons are drawn through the meat about 1 inch apart. If you don't have a larding needle you can lay the strips of bacon on the meat about an inch apart and bind them to the meat with twine.

Season with salt and pepper and roast slowly at 350 degrees. If you use a meat thermometer the meat will be done when the thermometer reads 140 degrees. This is the reading for rare beef.

A friend, carried away (to my delight) by my injunction to treat a good roast of venison like a good roast of beef, asked if I would give him my recipe for Yorkshire pudding. No, I wouldn't — and I won't include it here. Since you have removed most of the fat there are very few drippings, and even if you do like the taste of the fat you wouldn't use it for Yorkshire pudding as it behaves like lamb fat rather than beef fat.

Stuffed Venison Heart

A good-sized venison heart is about the same in size and tenderness as a calf's heart, and may be used in recipes calling for calf heart. It will serve three or four people, as the stuffing and gravy make this rather a hearty dish.

1 venison heart	1 teaspoon minced onion
1 cup bread crumbs	1 teaspoon chopped parsley
¼ cup melted butter, bacon or chicken fat	salt and pepper fat for frying

Cut out the veins and arteries and wash the heart in cold water. (To allay any fear that it will be tough, soak it overnight in water to which you have added 2 tablespoons of vinegar.)

Stuffed Cabbage Leaves

This is a good recipe if you're not in a tearing hurry. It is a bit tedious to wrap the meat mixture in the cabbage leaves, but the result is worth the extra effort.

1 large head of cabbage	1 green pepper, chopped
1 pound ground venison steak or stew meat	1 tablespoon parsley, chopped
1 pound ground lean pork	½ cup red wine
fat for frying	1 cup cooked rice
1 large onion, sliced	2 egg yolks
1 clove garlic, chopped fine	1 can tomatoes
½ cup celery, chopped	1 tablespoon flour

Prepare the cabbage leaves by taking 12 to 15 of the largest and soaking them in boiling water for 5 minutes. Cut out the hard rib at the base of the leaf so that it will roll easily. Drain the leaves on a towel and dry them gently.

Sauté the onion and garlic in olive oil, bacon fat or other shortening. Add the green pepper and the celery and cook a few minutes longer. Combine the venison and pork, adding the rice and the sautéed vegetables. Season well with salt, freshly-ground pepper, and herbs if you wish. Bind the mixture with the egg yolks, which have been slightly beaten with a fork. Divide into 12 portions and form into oblong rolls so that they can be rolled up in the prepared cabbage leaves. Tie with heavy thread, or fasten with toothpicks. Brown the rolls in butter or olive oil. Remove the rolls from the skillet and place them in the bottom of a casserole or fireproof dish. (You may now remove the fastenings, being careful not to let the leaves unroll.) Thicken the fat in the skillet with the flour and add the tomatoes and wine. When thickened, pour over the cabbage rolls, cover and cook in a moderate oven (350 degrees) for 1 hour or longer. Soured cream may be added a few minutes before removing the casserole from the oven.

Potato pancakes are good with this. *Gemütlich.*

Venison Curry

Curries are a matter of taste, and whether you like yours hot enough to burn your tongue or on the mild side, you will find that venison makes a very good curry. This is my idea of a moderately hot one. You may use uncooked meat or heat left-over roasted meat in the curry sauce.

1 pound venison, cut in 1½ inch cubes	¼ can tomato paste
1 onion, peeled and sliced	1 lime (*or lemon*)
1 clove garlic, sliced thin	½ pint water or beef stock
1 tablespoon (*more or less*) curry powder	butter or oil for frying

Fry the onion and garlic gently in butter or oil. Add the curry powder, stir and continue to fry for 2 or 3 minutes. (It is one of the secrets of good curry making to fry the curry powder; this releases the flavor and improves the taste of the dish.) Add the meat pieces and cook for a few minutes longer. Add the tomato paste and water or stock. Cover the pan and simmer over a low flame until the meat is tender and the gravy thick. It is better if you do not have to thicken the gravy with flour, but if it is too thin, a little flour or cornstarch mixed to a paste with water or wine may be used. Add salt and the juice of a fresh lime to taste.

Rice, of course, and chutney, either Major Grey's or Green Label Mango Chutney. In addition, you may serve any number of condiments and "fixings" as accompaniments to the curry. Here are some of them: grated carrot; finely chopped peanuts; chopped green pepper; Bombay Duck, if you can get it. And, best of all, bananas, sautéed in butter and dredged with sugar and a squeeze of lime or lemon juice.

Cornish Pasties

Cornish pasties are individual meat tarts and can be served either hot or cold. They are a good way to use trimmings of steak because the meat is cut in small pieces. They freeze well. You might try them for picnics or school lunches. They pack easily and are more satisfying than sandwiches. The following ingredients will make about 4 of the pasties and will give you an idea of the proportions so that you can make as many or as few as you like.

flaky pastry (using about 2 cups
    of flour)
½ pound venison steak
1 veal or 2 lamb kidneys
½ pound potatoes
1 tablespoon onion, finely chopped
salt and pepper

Cut the steak, kidney and peeled potatoes into cubes (1 inch or less), add the chopped onion and season to taste with salt and pepper.

Roll out the pastry (a fairly short pastry is best) and cut into rounds about 6 inches in diameter or in squares if you prefer. Put ¼ of the meat mixture on each round and fold over to make a half-circle, crimping the edges together and pressing firmly with the tines of a fork. Brush over the pasties with slightly beaten egg yolk if you like a glazed effect. Bake for 10 minutes in a fairly hot oven (425 degrees), then reduce the heat to 350 degrees and bake about 50 minutes more.

Don't try to make the pasties with meat or potato which has been cooked; it isn't the same thing at all.

N.B.: To answer a question often asked: *Pasty* rhymes with "nasty," not with "tasty." This is unfortunate because they are very tasty, easy to prepare, and economical!

Venison Mincemeat

This recipe was extracted with some difficulty from a Vermonter who hadn't reckoned to let it go out of the family. Some of her reluctance was based on the suspicion that the recipe might be used as evidence of possession of illegal deer! It makes enough mincemeat for about 15 pies. You might like to make a winter's supply and freeze it. The recipe can be halved or quartered very easily.

Do you know the story of the woman who pricked a "T" on all her pies before putting them on the attic stairs to freeze? She wanted to be able to tell the mince from the apple: "T" for " 'tis mince" and "T" for " 'taint mince"!

4 pounds venison (*scraps are fine for this*)
2 pounds beef suet
tart apples
3 pounds brown sugar
2 cups maple syrup (*or dark molasses*)
2 quarts cider
3 pounds currants
4 pounds seeded raisins

½ pound citron, cut fine
1 quart applejack (*or brandy, wine, cider or grape juice*)
1 tablespoon cinnamon
1 tablespoon ground clove
1 teaspoon allspice
1 teaspoon mace
1 teaspoon ground nutmeg
salt to taste

Cover the meat and suet with boiling water and cook until the meat is tender. Let it cool in the liquid. When it is cold and the fat has solidified, remove the meat and chop the cake fat (suet). Reboil the liquid until it is reduced to 1½ cups. Chop the venison and add to it twice as much apple, peeled, cored and chopped fine. Add the sugar and syrup or molasses, the dried fruits, the suet, the cider and the reduced liquid in which the meat was cooked. Boil slowly for 2 hours, stirring to prevent burning. Add the applejack or brandy and the spices. Mix thoroughly and store in crocks or jars.

It is by no means necessary to use exactly the ingredients given. You may want to add orange or lemon peel or chopped figs; or you may prefer a different proportion of spices. You may also use wine or sherry in place of the cider; or grape juice instead of the applejack or brandy.

Pot Roast with Vegetables

I can't think of a more satisfying dinner for a closed-in winter evening than one of venison pot roast, served in a ring of its own vegetables with plenty of crusty French bread. It can hold its own as a "company" dish, and has an added attraction in that it doesn't require intense last-minute attention.

3- to 4-pound pot roast	1 teaspoon parsley flakes
¼ cup salt pork, cubed small	¼ teaspoon thyme
2 tablespoons butter	1 cup dry white wine (*or red,*
6 carrots	*if you don't mind the pinkish*
6 small onions	*tinge to the vegetables*)
6 small potatoes	salt and pepper
1 stalk celery	1½ cups hot water

Lard your roast well by inserting the cubes of salt pork into crevices in the meat. Heat butter in a Dutch oven or deep casserole and brown the meat on all sides. Add the hot water, wine, carrots, onions, celery, parsley, thyme and salt and pepper. Cover and cook gently for 3 hours on top of the stove or in the oven, or until the meat is tender. (Simmering is important: it keeps the meat tender and juicy and prevents the vegetables from disintegrating.) If the liquid gets too low, add water, or

VENISON RECIPES

water and wine in the proportion you started with. About 30
minutes before the meal is to be served add the potatoes, peeled
and halved, correcting the seasoning since potatoes tend to
draw saltiness from the liquid. When the potatoes are done, remove the meat and the vegetables, discarding the celery if it is
bedraggled. If necessary, reduce the liquid rapidly over high
heat while keeping the pot roast and the vegetables hot. Ar-
range the meat and vegetables on a deep hot platter, pour some
of the pot-liquor over the top, put the rest in a gravy boat, and
serve.

VARIETY MEATS

The term "variety meats" to designate hearts, liver, kidneys,
fresh tongue, brains and sweetbreads always strikes me as odd,
although it is a great improvement over the word "offal," which
is the way they are described in England. (Where they *are*
eaten in spite of the name.)

The chief reason we don't think of them in connection with
venison is that they are small, and most hunting households
have only one deer a year at their disposal. These meats are
perfectly edible, however, and if you have a small family or
several successful hunters and therefore several deer, you may
want to try them.

Liver

Venison liver is considered an especial delicacy, and if you like
liver you will not need to be urged to serve it. Many hunters
cook and eat the liver right after the animal is killed, as it is at
its best when very fresh; we always have the liver for dinner to

celebrate our luck. It can be frozen, but should not be kept longer than 3 or 4 months.

Cook it just as you would calf's liver. I have never been an exponent of boiling liver, dredging it and then frying it. One of the quickest and tastiest ways I know of to treat liver is to skin the slices, removing the veins; cutting it into strips 1½ inch long and ½ inch wide. Heat butter in a heavy skillet, scrape a little onion pulp into the butter and let it cook gently for a moment to release the flavor. Toss in the pieces of liver, sauté them briskly for the equivalent of 1 minute on either side, season with salt and pepper and serve directly from the pan.

Boiled Fresh Tongue

Wash the tongue and soak in cold water for 1 hour. Put it in a saucepan and cover with water to which you have added:

1 clove garlic	2 stalks of celery cut in pieces
1 bay leaf	1 teaspoon salt
1 small onion sliced thin	4 peppercorns

Simmer until tongue is tender (2 hours or more). Drain and cool. Skin tongue, removing roots and trimming it to look neat. Chill and slice before serving.

Brains

Soak brains in cold water for 1 hour. Remove membrane and any blood clots. Parboil 5 minutes in salted water to which you have added 1 tablespoon of vinegar or white wine. Drain and cut into cubes. Melt butter in a skillet and, when bubbling, add brains. Let the butter get quite brown; add a squeeze of lemon or lime juice and serve *immediately* on toast.

Kidneys

The kidneys may be broiled or sautéed in butter with a dash of white wine or sherry; or they may be added to any stew, or chopped fine and added to gravy.

Mix the crumbs, melted butter, onion and parsley lightly with a fork, seasoning to taste. You may add any herbs you wish: basil or marjoram are good. Stuff the heart, sprinkle with salt and pepper and dredge with flour. Melt fat in a skillet and brown the heart. Put it in a casserole or covered baking dish and half cover with boiling water or stock, adding ½ cup red wine if you wish. Cover and bake for 2 hours in a moderate oven. When the heart is tender, remove it from the casserole and keep hot while you are thickening the gravy with flour mixed with a little cold water or wine. Re-season if necessary.

Rice or noodles are good with this, since there should be plenty of gravy. Adding ½ cup of currant jelly to the gravy after thickening gives a delicious flavor.

As an alternative, try stuffing the heart with a combination of dried prunes and apricots. The prunes should be pitted, of course, and each dried apricot half should be cut in two pieces.

SOME CALL IT STEW

Venison Stroganoff

This is an elegant dish for a party. It is convenient too, for some people insist that it is even better when made beforehand and re-heated. The trick is to use the very best and tenderest steak, as the meat should not be overcooked.

1½ pounds venison steak
½ pound mushrooms
3 tablespoons butter

½ pint soured cream
1 tablespoon flour
salt and paprika to taste

Cut the steak in thin strips about ¼ inch wide and 1 inch long. It should be cut *across* the grain; this makes it even more tender.

Melt the butter in a heavy frying pan or skillet, one that has a cover. When the butter is bubbling add the cut-up steak and cook slowly, covered. The meat should be stirred occasionally. At the end of 15 minutes add the mushrooms which have been peeled and broken into rather small pieces. Cover and cook the meat and mushrooms for 10 minutes longer.

Now put the meat and mushroom mixture into the top of a double boiler over a low flame. Melt another tablespoon of butter in the frying pan, and when it is melted add the flour. When the flour and butter are smooth add the soured cream and stir over a very low flame for 3 or 4 minutes. Pour the sauce over the meat mixture in the double boiler and simmer for 10 to 15 minutes. Season to taste with salt and paprika. Do not overseason; the flavor of the steak, mushrooms and butter should not be lost.

Serve the Stroganoff in a ring of boiled rice, with noodles, or on baking powder biscuits. The biscuits should be larger than usual, about 3 inches in diameter. If you are going all out, you can make rounds of puff-pastry about 3 inches in diameter, heap the meat mixture on the pastry and top with smaller rounds of puff-pastry, about 1 inch in diameter.

Sauerbraten

Here's where you marinate! Personally I don't get hysterical at the thought of ginger snaps in the gravy; you may do as you choose about this.

3–4 pound piece of venison
    (*the neck may be used*)
salt pork for larding
1 onion, peeled and sliced
1 clove garlic
¼ cup sugar
12 whole cloves
1 teaspoon peppercorns

1 tablespoon dry English mustard
salt
vinegar (*tarragon is good*) and
    water in equal parts to
    half-cover the meat
1 cup soured cream
4 ginger snaps (*maybe*)
fat for frying

Lard the meat by threading it in several places with thin strips of salt pork drawn by a larding needle. If this seems too difficult you may omit the larding; it won't make too much difference. Put the meat in an earthenware crock or bowl. Heat (do not boil) the vinegar and water, add the seasonings and pour over the meat. Cover and let stand from 4 to 8 days, turning the meat once or twice each day. Remove the meat from the marinade, rub with garlic and dredge well with flour. Melt the fat in a Dutch oven or deep heavy saucepan with a tight-fitting cover. Brown the meat on all sides, pour the marinade over it, cover closely, and simmer over a low flame for 2 to 3 hours, or until tender. When the meat is done remove it from the pan and keep it hot while you thicken the gravy with flour mixed with water or wine to make a thin paste. Now is the time to add the ginger snaps if you can bring yourself to do it! Just before serving add the soured cream and pour the gravy over the meat.

I know that potato dumplings are *de rigueur* with Sauerbraten, but I often serve buttered noodles; and I like coleslaw with thin slices of tart apple with this.

Venison Stew

This is a recipe for venison stew exactly as it was written down and given to me by my rich aunt, who is well known for the excellence of her table.

2 pounds of venison cut in
   1½ inch cubes
2 onions, quartered
1 lemon, sliced
1½ cups red wine
   (*it needn't be* drinkable)

1 bay leaf (*I don't like it*)
1 teaspoon thyme
1/3 cup chopped parsley
salt and pepper
3 tablespoons fat (*not venison fat*)

Put all the ingredients except the fat into a deep crock and marinate overnight. Drain off the marinade and save.

Sauté the meat in the fat in an uncovered pressure saucepan until golden brown. Add the marinade, cover and cook under 15 pounds pressure for 45 minutes; reduce the pressure gradually. Or, if you use a covered Dutch oven, simmer for 2½ hours. Serves four, or six if they have moderate appetites.

Serve with watercress and avocado salad, dressed with fresh

lime juice. French bread, unsalted butter and good strong coffee are all you need with this.

Venison Goulasch

Whether you spell it Goulash, Goulasch, or Gulyas, this old Hungarian stand-by is a hearty, satisfying dish. It can be prepared beforehand and re-heated. Moreover, the less tender cuts of meat are generally used, so that it is a favorite with busy and/or thrifty cooks.

2 pounds venison cut in
1½ inch cubes
3 tablespoons flour
3 tablespoons bacon fat, beef suet, or olive oil
2 cloves garlic
1 large onion, sliced or chopped fine
1 tablespoon paprika (*if you can get real Hungarian Rosen paprika so much the better*)

½ cup red wine
1 quart boiling water or stock
salt
tomato paste (small can) and canned tomatoes may be added; if canned tomatoes are used, the amount of water or stock should be reduced.

Roll pieces of meat in flour, pressing flour into them. Melt fat in skillet and cook onion slowly until transparent and golden brown. Add meat, browning well. Add seasonings and liquid. Stir well and cover. Cook slowly until meat is very tender — 2 or 3 hours. More stock, water, or wine may be added if it boils away, although slow cooking should prevent this. Soured cream may be added to the Goulasch just before serving.

This dish may also be cooked in a pressure pan. If you use a pressure saucepan, melt the fat and brown the onion and meat in the pan, adding only *1 cup* of liquid. Cook for 25 minutes under 15 pounds pressure.

Buttered noodles, the "broad" kind, are the usual accompaniment to Goulasch. Less usual but delicious: boiled new potatoes with soured cream poured over them just before serving.

As another vegetable, red cabbage cooked with apple is excellent.

FINE BUT UNCLASSIFIED

Chinese Pepper Steak

The Chinese use beefsteak in this, but it is excellent made with venison. It is a good way of using a thin piece of steak, perhaps one that is too irregular in shape to be served whole. In these days, bean sprouts can be bought in cans in almost every grocery, and so can the soya sauce and the Chinese noodles to serve with it. The only ingredient that may prove difficult to track down is the ginger root. It is an addition if you can find it, but not essential to the dish.

1 pound thin steak	¼ cup sherry, vermouth or water
3 tablespoons olive oil or butter	3 scallions or the equivalent in
1 clove garlic, mashed	onion tops, cut in thin rings
1 teaspoon green ginger root,	1 can bean sprouts
mashed (*if you can get it*)	2 tomatoes
3 tablespoons soya sauce	2 green peppers, sliced thin
1 teaspoon sugar	salt and pepper
3 tablespoons cornstarch	

Slice the steak across the grain as thin as possible. Cook the steak in the oil or butter with the garlic and ginger root in a skillet over a medium flame for 10 minutes. Add the green pepper and the tomatoes, skinned and sliced, cover and cook over a low flame for a further 5 minutes. Add the bean sprouts, cover and let simmer a few minutes. Mix the cornstarch with wine or water and pour over the mixture in the skillet. Season with salt, pepper and soya sauce. Remember that the soya sauce is salty, and reduce the salt to taste. Do *not* overcook: the pepper steak is done when the cornstarch has thickened. Add the scallions or onion tops 1 minute before serving.

Serve the pepper steak with rice and Chinese noodles (canned), which have been crisped in the oven for a few minutes. A bottle of soya sauce should be on the table. Chinese dishes do not require vegetables or salad served separately. Be sure to have plenty of rice, and see that your rice is cooked so that each grain is separate. The pre-cooked rice will not do with Chinese food. A compote of stewed fruit, rhubarb stewed with thin slices of orange, or the Chinese favorite, kumquats in syrup, are all excellent desserts with this meal. Tea without lemon or cream, or white wine, may be served with the main course.

Venison and Kidney Pie

Unfavorable opinions of English cooking are based largely on experiences with the English way with vegetables, a surfeit of suet puddings, a run-in, perhaps, with Toad-in-the-hole, and above all the monotony of the menu. But, England has always been noted for its roasts and chops, meat pies, and especially for its game cookery. Venison and kidney pie may dispel some of your prejudices on this score.

1 pound stewing steak, cut in 1½ inch cubes	3 medium onions, peeled and sliced salt and pepper
1 beef kidney or 8 lamb kidneys	boiling water or stock
3 tablespoons fat (*beef suet may be used*)	piecrust
	1 egg yolk (*optional*)

Prepare the kidneys by removing the membrane and cutting out the white part. Slice the beef kidney or halve the lamb kidneys. Roll steak and kidney pieces in flour, pressing the flour into the meat. Melt the fat in a skillet and brown the pieces of meat. Put the meat and onions into a fairly deep fireproof dish (the dish should be about ¾ full). Put the boiling water or stock into the skillet to take up all the gravy and cover the meat in the dish with this mixture. Put on the lid and bake in a medium oven (350 degrees) for at least 1 hour — or until the meat is tender and the gravy thick. Add salt and pepper to taste. If you are in a hurry, this part of the cooking can be done in a pressure saucepan. Cook the meat about 20 minutes under 15 pounds pressure. Remember to reduce the liquid by about ½ the amount recommended for baking. When the meat is cooked (either method), remove from the oven — or, if pressure cooked, put meat in baking dish — and cover with crust, fluting the edges and making several slashes in the crust to let out the steam. (The English cut a round hole about 1 inch in diameter in the center of the crust.) Brush the crust with an egg yolk beaten up in 1 tablespoon of water if you like a shiny crust. Bake in a hot oven (400 degrees) until the crust is nicely browned.

Why not go the whole hog and serve boiled potatoes and brussels sprouts? The potatoes might be tiny new ones, boiled in their skins. If you are cooking brussels sprouts, remove them from the fire while they are still firm, sauté them in butter just before serving and there will be no rude remarks.

CHAPTER VII

The Company It Keeps

TO MY MIND much of the festivity occasioned by serving fine venison comes from the dishes that accompany it. There are many such good companions, a number of them traditional and ranging from simple vegetables right on through wild currant jelly and conserves that now abound on the specialty shelves of your local grocery.

You can take off happily to plan your own menus from these two generalities:

1. With broiled or roast venison serve any vegetable you would normally have with meats of this texture and cooked in this manner.

2. With venison stews you can limit yourself to a starch vegetable or a paste to catch the sauce, a tossed salad and French bread.

Steaks, chops and roasts are well set off by potatoes presented in a number of ways, by grilled or baked tomatoes, eggplant, corn fritters, baked or boiled onions, turnips, cabbage, beets. Perhaps you wouldn't bother with wild rice and mushrooms or puréed chestnuts or Cumberland sauce with a routine meal. But think of them now, for theirs is an old affinity for venison and you are planning a gala dinner.

Before I go on with a few recipes for my own favorites I shall comment briefly on salads, breads, garnishes, desserts and wines.

SALADS

The simpler the salad the better. You can never go wrong with your best one of tossed greens; especially since venison is felt to be a man's meat, the salad should be kept very straightforward. Depending upon the heartiness of appetites, you could have a Caesar salad variation with a one-minute egg and croutons tossed with the greens at the last moment. Fruit and lettuce confections are unnecessary with a good venison dinner: much better and easier to save fruit for the end of the meal. Green salads should, I feel, be served separately after the main course.

Coleslaws are good with venison, too, and my own reaction is that they should not be so overpoweringly seasoned that they war with the meat flavors you have been at such pains to preserve or enhance. These can be served along with the main course.

BREADS

I seldom have any bread with venison except good chunks from a crisp French loaf, or crisp rolls. The exceptions are biscuits, served sometimes with the Stroganoff, and a good, rough, unsweetened johnny-cake to please one of my pet guests when I have pot roast. As for having sweet rolls or other quick breads than these, I don't.

GARNISHES

There is great variety here, led by currant jelly: good conserves, spiced crabapples, chutneys, your own best pickle relishes, horseradish sauce are a few of them. There is no need for carrot sticks or stuffed celery. And I have said my say about catsup and chili sauce.

DESSERTS

The desserts you serve with venison dinners depend upon whether or not you have shot your bolt in preparing the main part of the meal. I usually taper off by serving green salad, then offering fresh fruit or a good fruit compote, cheese — Brie, Gruyère, Roquefort or Bleu, Camembert — and unsalted crackers and coffee. Occasionally I have hot gingerbread with chunks of Cheddar cheese to eat with it (we in Vermont are blessed with a wonderful "store cheese" of this sort: Crowley's Mount Holly cheese). The soft ripened cheeses, by the way, should appear on the table at room temperature, never fresh from the refrigerator.

WINES

If you take wine with meals you will certainly insist upon it now. Aside from the fact that you can't go wrong serving a good dry red wine with venison, the only limitations are the degree of your connoisseurship and the size of your pocketbook. You can range from the finest imported Burgundies and such names as Chambertin, Beaune, Beaujolais, Chateauneuf-du-Pape, to very good domestic red wines from the Napa Valley and Peninsula regions of Northern California. Red wine is served at room temperature.

* * *

Coleslaw with Tart Apple

[GOOD WITH SAUERBRATEN]

Shred one firm medium cabbage and add to it 2 medium, thin-sliced apples as tart as you can get them. Mix the cabbage with your best French dressing, adding the apples just before serving so they will not have a chance to discolor. You can use boiled dressing if you prefer, but its flavor should not be too sharp.

Squash

Squash — boiled, baked or fried in rings — goes well with venison. You can bake acorn squash in a good fashion by putting butter, salt, pepper and a generous tablespoon of maple syrup in each hollowed half before you put it into the oven. Or you may boil zucchini or summer squash, making certain that they are small and tender. Slice the squash thin and cook it with 1/3 cup of salted water in the pressure pan for 1 minute at 15 pounds pressure. Drain very well, add a good lump of butter and grate fresh nutmeg over the top.

Spinach does well topped with fresh nutmeg, too. Chopping the spinach fine makes it a better dish, I think.

Purée of Chestnuts

This is a seasonal dish, since chestnuts appear in most markets only about Thanksgiving or Christmas time (be leery of any that have been around a long time: they are likely to get moldy). I served puréed chestnuts as I would mashed potatoes, though with not such a lavish hand.

1 pound chestnuts	salt
2 teaspoons olive oil	pepper
butter	meat stock

I prefer to hull my chestnuts the following way, because I don't like any possible tannic flavor which might result if they were boiled in their shells: cut an "X" across the flat side of each nut, and place them in a heavy skillet in which you have heated the olive oil. Shake the nuts until they are well coated with oil, then place them, skillet and all, into a slow oven until the shells have curled back and they are roasted through. Remove from the oven; shell and peel them while they are still as warm as you can handle them; put the meats through a ricer or food mill, adding butter and hot meat stock almost drop by drop, until you have a good consistency. Season with a little salt and with freshly-ground pepper. Serves four.

Beets in Red Wine

Peel two bunches of beets and put them through a grinder (this is a messy job but the result is worth it). Sauté the ground beets in 4 tablespoons of melted butter into which you have scraped 1 teaspoon onion pulp, cooking slowly for 15 minutes. Add red wine to cover and continue cooking until tender. Serve topped with a generous dollop of soured cream or with chopped fresh parsley.

Tomatoes and Eggplant

1 medium eggplant	1 clove garlic, chopped fine
1 medium onion, sliced very thin	1 tablespoon sugar
1 can tomatoes	salt
1 tablespoon chopped parsley	pepper

Slice the eggplant, leaving on the skin, in pieces 1 inch thick. Put it right into the pressure pan, bring to 15 pounds pressure in 1/3 cup of water for 1 minute; remove and drain. Sauté the garlic and onion in butter or olive oil, add to them the can of tomatoes with its juice, the parsley, salt, pepper and sugar. Simmer this mixture 10 minutes. Add the eggplant, and turn the whole thing into a casserole. Cover with crumbs, dot with butter, bake in a 350° oven for 25 minutes.

Stewed Red Cabbage with Apple

This is good with Goulasch, or with any other dish of a similar consistency and flavor.

1 red cabbage	caraway seeds (*don't include them unless they are liked*)
1 tart apple, peeled and chopped	
1 medium onion, chopped finely	salt
red wine (*optional*)	

Cut your cabbage as you always do, add the apple and the onion and the caraway. Add only enough water to cook it, using red wine for part of the liquid if you wish. Season and cook slowly, covered — or in a pressure pan — until the cabbage is done to your taste. Serves 4 to 6 depending upon the size of the cabbage.

Wild Rice with Mushrooms

This goes well with a juicy roast, and needs only a fine green vegetable — spinach with nutmeg or frenched green beans with Hollandaise sauce — salad, cheese, fruit and coffee to be a perfect meal in my estimation.

1¼ cups wild rice	¼ cup butter
1 teaspoon salt	good meat broth
⅜ pound fresh mushrooms	

If you soak the rice overnight it need not be cooked in a double boiler, but may be cooked directly over the heat. At any rate, put the rice in a pan, pour over it 4 cups of boiling water, add the salt, and let it cook very, very gently for 30 minutes. When it is *almost* tender, drain away any water that may remain, substituting a cup of good meat stock — good strong bouillon may be used if you like. Put it back on the low heat. Meanwhile peel, slice and sauté the mushrooms in butter; season and add to the rice, letting them cook together for a few minutes. Serve rice mounded on a small, deep platter.

Potato Dumplings

6 medium potatoes, peeled, boiled and cooled	½ cup flour
	pinch of nutmeg
2 eggs	pinch of cinnamon } *I usually omit these*
1 teaspoon salt	¼ cup butter

Mash cold potatoes thoroughly and put them on a bread-board, rolling them if necessary to remove any lumps. Make a well in the center of the potatoes and add the unbeaten eggs and salt and enough flour to make the mixture easy to handle without making it stiff. Knead lightly until smooth, form into a roll about 2 inches in diameter; cut 1-inch slices from the roll, form them into balls, and put them into a large pan of boiling water you have salted as you do for noodles. The pan should be large enough so that the dumplings do not touch as they cook. Boil gently for 15 minutes, drain thoroughly and keep warm. Pour the butter, which you have melted, over them just before serving. These dumplings can be garnished with crumbs or croutons, but I prefer them just with butter.

Hollandaise Sauce

I was given this "way" — she never called anything a "recipe" — for making Hollandaise sauce by Isolina Roncarati, the finest factotum in a kitchen I have ever known. She never heard of "mock" Hollandaise, and never, so far as I know, had to bind her sauce. The secret is never to let it get too hot.

3 teaspoons (that's what she says) fresh lemon juice	¼ pound butter
	salt
2 unbeaten egg yolks	freshly ground pepper

Add the egg yolks to the lemon juice, along with salt and pepper; stir roughly once or twice to break the yolks so they won't form a skin if you are doing this in advance. Have your butter well softened — but never melted. Put lemon-egg mixture into a deep crock over gently boiling water. Start beating with a rotary beater, and add the butter one third at a time. When the butter is consumed, continue beating until the sauce begins to stiffen. Remove the crock from the water, dry it, and carry the sauce to the table in it.

Cumberland Sauce

Melt 4 tablespoons of good red currant jelly in a saucepan and add ¼ cup of consommé, 2 tablespoons of tomato sauce and 1 tablespoon of port wine. Boil 2 tablespoons of dried currants for just a few minutes, or until they have softened, and add them to the sauce. Add 1½ tablespoons of sliced blanched almonds. Boil gently for 15 minutes, stirring occasionally; serve in a small sauceboat.

Index

Antlers, 15, 31

Bladder, removal of, 18
Bleeding, 14
Bread, 71
Butchering, 32-40
Butter, flavored, 53, 54

Canning, 7; see also Pressure canning
Carcass, halving, 32, 33, 38, 39;
    quartering, 33-39
Carrying, see Transporting
Chops, 35, 39, 52, 53
Cleaning, 19, 40
Cooling, 19, 20, 27
Curing, 46, 47

Dessert, 71, 72
Dragging, see Transporting
Dressing, see Hog-dressing

Fat, 50, 52, 56
Flavor, gamy, 8, 25, 26, 50
Freezing, 26, 27, 41, 42

Garnishes, 49, 71
Glands, scent, 29
Gutting, 18, 19; see also Hog-dressing

Hamburger, 35, 39, 40
Hanging, 25-28
Head, mounting, see Antlers
Herbs, 48, 49
Hide, curing of, 30, 31
Hog-dressing, 13-20

Jerky, 47

Kidneys, 40, 62, 63
Killing, 10-13
Knives, 13, 14, 32

Laws, game, 13, 24, 25
Liver, 19, 39, 40, 61, 62

Marinades, 50-52
Mincemeat, 36, 59, 60

Pickling, 46, 47
Pressure canning, 43-46

Recipes, to go with venison:
    Beets in red wine, 74
    Coleslaw with apple, 72
    Cumberland sauce, 77

Hollandaise sauce, 76, 77
    Potato dumplings, 76
    Puree of chestnuts, 73, 74
    Squash, 73
    Stewed cabbage with apple, 74, 75
    Tomatoes and eggplant, 74
    Wild rice with mushrooms, 75
Recipes, venison:
    Brains, 62
    Chinese pepper steak, 67, 68
    Chops, 52, 53
    Cornish pasties, 58
    Gespickter Rehfleisch, 55
    Kidneys, 62, 63
    Liver, 61, 62
    Pot roast with vegetables, 60, 61
    Roasts, 54-56, 60, 61
    Sauerbraten, 64, 65
    Steaks, 52, 53
    Stuffed cabbage leaves, 56, 57
    ——heart, 56
    Tongue, 62
    Variety meats, 61-63
    Venison and kidney pie, 68, 69
    ——curry, 57, 58
    ——goulasch, 66
    ——mincemeat, 59, 60
    ——stew, 65, 66
    ——stroganoff, 63, 64
Roasts, 32, 35, 36, 38, 39, 54-56,
    60, 61

Salad, 71
Sauces, 49, 53, 76, 77
Sausage, 40
Skinning, 28-31
Smoking, 46, 47
Spices, 49
Spoilage, 27, 43
Steaks, 38, 39, 52, 53
Stew, 35, 36, 39, 63-66
Sticking, 14, 15

Tenderizing, 25-27, 50
Transporting, 21-25

Variety meats, 40, 61-63
Venison, enjoyment of, 8, 40

Weight, dressed, 39
Wine, 49, 72